W9-AEA-350

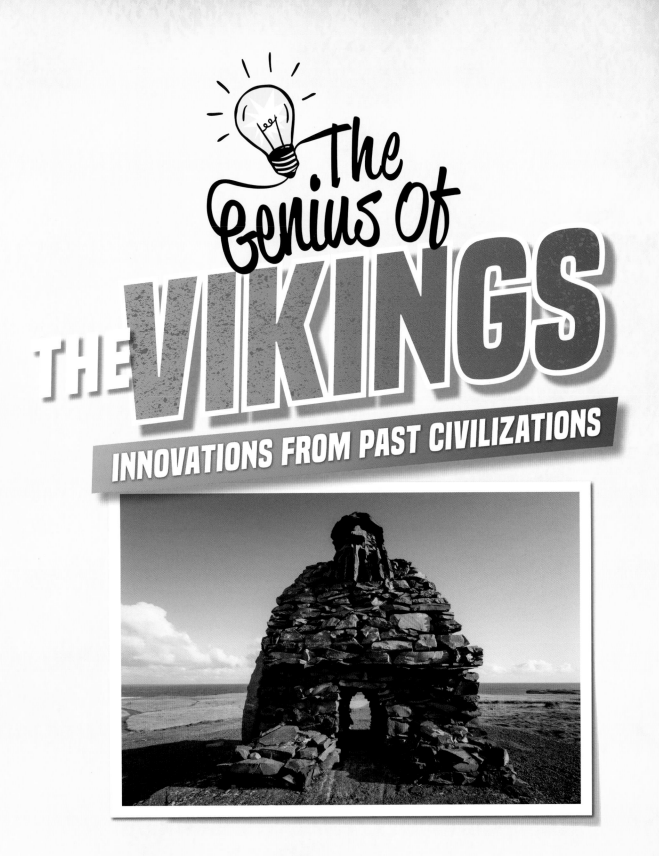

The Genius Of THE VIKINGS

INNOVATIONS FROM PAST CIVILIZATIONS

SONYA NEWLAND

CRABTREE
PUBLISHING COMPANY
WWW.CRABTREEBOOKS.COM

CRABTREE
PUBLISHING COMPANY
WWW.CRABTREEBOOKS.COM

Published in Canada
Crabtree Publishing
616 Welland Avenue
St. Catharines, ON
L2M 5V6

Published in the United States
Crabtree Publishing
PMB 59051
350 Fifth Ave, 59th Floor
New York, NY 10118

Published in 2020 by Crabtree Publishing Company

First published in Great Britain in 2019 by The Watts Publishing Group
Copyright © The Watts Publishing Group 2019

Author: Sonya Newland

Editorial director: Kathy Middleton

Editors: Sonya Newland, Petrice Custance

Proofreader: Melissa Boyce

Series designer: Rocket Design (East Anglia) Ltd

Designer: Clare Nicholas

Prepress technician: Tammy McGarr

Print coordinator: Katherine Berti

Consultant: Philip Parker

Printed in the U.S.A./072019/CG20190501

Photo credits:
Alamy: Heritage Image Partnership Ltd cover, 21, Chronicle 5, National Geographic Creative 15, Dorling Kindersley Ltd 22, North Wind Picture Archives 24, Art Collection 3 25, Prisma Archivo 26; Julian Baker: 6–7, 10, 12; Getty Images: Andy Crawford 4, Heritage Images 13b, Werner Forman 14r, 28; iStock: gremlin 11b, Himagine 13t, Elenarts 18, Tony Baggett 27; Shutterstock: goga18128 7, Algol 8, lovelypeace 9, Aleksandr Pobedimskiy 11t, Tony Baggett 14l, yanami 16–17, GTS Productions 19, elxeneize 20, Drakuliren 23, Alexander A.Trofimov 29.

All design elements from Shutterstock.

Every attempt has been made to clear copyright. Should there be any inadvertent omission please apply to the publisher for rectification.

The website addresses (URLs) included in this book were valid at the time of going to press. However, it is possible that contents or addresses may have changed since the publication of this book. No responsibility for any such changes can be accepted by either the author or the Publisher.

Library and Archives Canada Cataloguing in Publication

Title: The genius of the Vikings / Sonya Newland.
Names: Newland, Sonya, author.
Series: Genius of the ancients.
Description: Series statement: The genius of the ancients | Includes index.
Identifiers: Canadiana (print) 20190108576 |
  Canadiana (ebook) 20190108584 |
  ISBN 9780778765905 (hardcover) |
  ISBN 9780778765981 (softcover) |
  ISBN 9781427123954 (HTML)
Subjects: LCSH: Vikings—Juvenile literature. | LCSH: Civilization, Viking—Juvenile literature.
Classification: LCC DL66 .N49 2019 | DDC j948/.022—dc23

Library of Congress Cataloging-in-Publication Data

Names: Newland, Sonya, author.
Title: The genius of the Vikings / Sonya Newland.
Description: New York : Crabtree Publishing, [2019] |
  Series: The Genius of the Ancients | Includes index.
Identifiers: LCCN 2019014242 (print) | LCCN 2019016146 (ebook) |
  ISBN 9781427123954 (Electronic) |
  ISBN 9780778765905 (hardcover) |
  ISBN 9780778765981 (pbk.)
Subjects: LCSH: Vikings--Juvenile literature.
Classification: LCC DL66 (ebook) | LCC DL66 .N48 2019 (print) |
  DDC 948/.022--dc23
LC record available at https://lccn.loc.gov/2019014242

CONTENTS

THE VIKINGS ———————————————— 4

THE VIKING LONGSHIP ——————————— 6

SAILS AND KEELS —————————————— 8

COMPASSES ————————————————— 10

EXPLORATION ————————————————— 12

TRADE ————————————————————— 14

BATTLE-AXES ————————————————— 16

SHIELDS —————————————————————— 18

LAW AND DEMOCRACY ————————————— 20

LANGUAGE ————————————————————— 22

SKIING —————————————————————— 24

PERSONAL GROOMING ————————————— 26

VIKING SAGAS ————————————————— 28

GLOSSARY ———————————————————— 30

TIMELINE ————————————————————— 31

INDEX AND LEARNING MORE ————————— 32

THE VIKINGS

Who?

The "people from the north" came from the part of northern Europe we call Scandinavia, which includes Denmark, Norway, and Sweden. Known as Norse people, *norse* being the Norwegian word for north, they were farmers, fishers, and skilled sailors. In the 700s, they began sailing along the coast of Europe, **raiding** and stealing from many settlements. This behavior may have earned them the nickname *vikingr*, which means **pirate** in the **Old Norse language**. Today, we refer to them as Vikings.

Viking helmets did not have horns, although they are often shown with horns in modern pictures.

What happened?

The Vikings began raiding coastal villages in England in the late 700s. At first, they simply took what they wanted and sailed away. But by around 850, Vikings were settling in England. In 886, the English king Alfred reached an agreement with the Vikings. They would be allowed to live in a certain part of the country. This large area under Viking **influence** became known as the Danelaw.

Despite this early agreement, over the next 200 years there were many shifts in power as the **Anglo-Saxons** and the Vikings fought fiercely over control of England. The Viking Age is considered to have ended in 1066, when the French duke William of Normandy invaded and conquered England.

During this time, the Vikings were also raiding, trading, and settling in other parts of the world. Their **legacy** can be seen far and wide.

This picture shows King Alfred's ships fighting the Vikings at sea. The two sides eventually reached an agreement.

THE VIKING LONGSHIP

The Vikings are most famous for their lightweight wooden boats, called longships. These cleverly designed vessels allowed the Vikings to travel farther and faster than almost anyone else at the time.

GENIUS
STATE-OF-THE-ART SHIPS

How long were longships?

According to writings, one of the longest and most powerful Viking longships was called *The Long Serpent*, or *Ormen Lange* in Norwegian. It was described as being more than 145 feet (44 m) long, with 34 pairs of oars. That's longer than four buses end to end! A typical longship was about 65 to 75 feet (20 to 23 m) in length. The Vikings built their ships with shallow **hulls**, which meant they could travel in shallow water, such as rivers. This allowed them to make surprise raids in places no one expected them to reach.

sail

figurehead

hull

A Viking crew

Longships had a row of oars on each side, usually powered by between 15 and 60 rowers. There were no cabins for the crew to take shelter in, so they ate and slept on deck. Each crew member had a chest to keep his belongings in. These may have doubled up as seats for the rowers. The longships were very light, so they could travel quickly and be moved easily by the rowers.

The Vikings may have believed that the dragon heads protected the ship and crew from evil spirits.

WOW!

The Vikings carved fierce-looking figureheads at the front and back of their longships. These were often in the shape of dragons, which is why longships are also sometimes called dragon ships.

oars

SAILS AND KEELS

At first, the Vikings just explored and raided coastal areas not far from their homeland. Later, they developed **technology** that improved their longships so that they could go much faster and travel farther than ever before.

GENIUS
★ OCEAN-GOING TECHNOLOGY ★

))) BRAIN WAVE)))

A kind of wooden pole called a beitass was attached to the lower corner of the sail. It helped to strengthen the sail against strong winds. The beitass also allowed the sail to be moved when the wind changed, to keep the ship sailing in the right direction.

Setting sail

Longships were not only powered by rowers. They also had a huge square sail, made of rough **woven** wool and attached to a tall **mast**. The sail could measure up to 36 feet (11 m) across, and it gave the longship much greater speed than rowers alone. The sail had the added advantage of allowing the Vikings to save their strength for the attack they would carry out when they reached their destination.

Some longships could reach top speeds of 17 miles per hour (28 kph).

Inventing the keel

Early Viking boats were not very stable, and often **capsized** in rough water. This changed with the **invention** of the keel, which was a strip of wood attached to the bottom of the longship. The keel made a longship much more stable, and allowed the Vikings to sail farther out to sea instead of being **confined** to rivers and coastlines. This opened up a whole new world to the Vikings, providing greater opportunities for exploration, raiding, and trade.

Most of what we know about longships comes from **archaeological** finds. This is the Oseberg ship, discovered in Norway.

WOW!

Vikings kept ravens in cages on longships. To check if they were near land, they would release the ravens. If the birds did not return, the Vikings knew land was nearby.

COMPASSES

To be successful explorers, raiders, and traders, the Vikings had to have good **navigational** aids. They invented an amazing device called a sun **compass** to help them find their way across the sea.

GENIUS ★ ★ NAVIGATIONAL INSTRUMENTS

Sailing by the Sun

A sun compass was a circular wooden disk with a hole in the middle. A peg called a gnomon was inserted in the hole so it stood upright. As the Sun fell on the gnomon, it created a shadow on the wooden disk. Sailors marked the position of the shadow every hour from sunrise to sunset. Then they drew a line to connect the points. This line showed the direction of north to south. The Vikings could then match up the Sun to the line on the compass to figure out their position while at sea.

north

shadow lines

gnomon

Part of a Viking sun compass was discovered in 1948. Experts have studied it to figure out how the Vikings used it to navigate.

WOW!

The Vikings realized they needed to **adapt** the sun compass to allow for the Sun being at different heights at different times of the year. They carried gnomons of different sizes to help them do this.

Knowledge of Earth

The **mineral** magnetite was plentiful in Scandinavia, and the Vikings may have used it to make a type of **magnetic** compass. Magnetite is naturally magnetic, and a piece of magnetite is called a lodestone. If a lodestone is hung and left to spin on its own, it will naturally point to the north-south line. The Vikings knew that the Sun rises in the east and sets in the west. They also knew that in their part of the world, the Sun was in the south at noon. This knowledge would have allowed them to figure out which end of the lodestone pointed north and which end pointed south.

In early English, "lode" meant "journey." The mineral may have gotten its name because of its early use in compasses.

EXPLORATION

The Vikings were among the first people to travel far from their homeland to discover and **colonize** other lands. They sailed east to what is now Russia and as far south as North Africa.

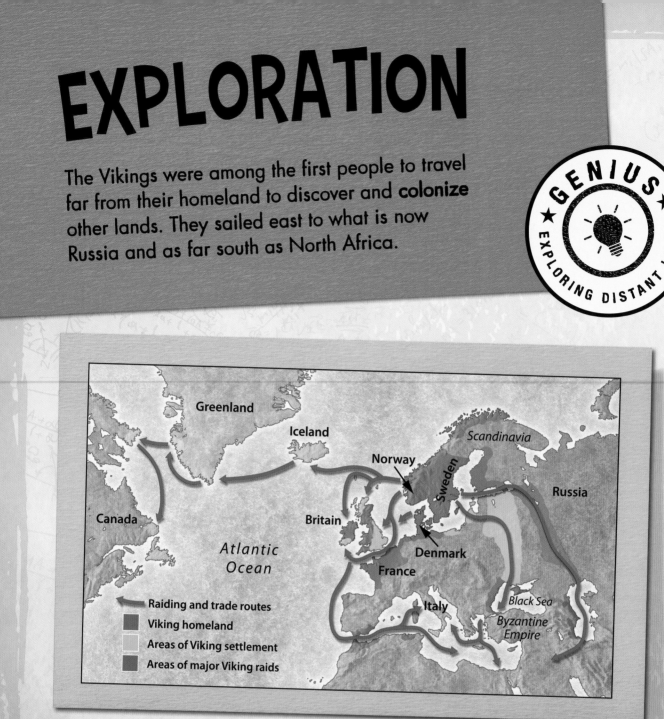

Exploring Iceland

One of the first countries the Vikings discovered was Iceland. It was first visited by a Viking named Naddodd around 850. In around 860, the Viking explorer Gardar Svavarsson sailed all the way around Iceland, proving it was an island. By 930, it is believed that about 30,000 people, but possibly as many as 70,000 people, had settled in Iceland.

At the height of the Vikings' power, their settlements could be found from North America to Russia.

Greenland

In around 980, a Viking named Erik the Red was banished from Iceland after he killed someone. After setting sail in 982, he arrived at a place he later called Greenland. He thought this pleasant name would make people want to live there. Erik was allowed to return to Iceland three years later. He encouraged other Vikings to go back to Greenland with him to explore and settle in this area.

A statue of Erik the Red in Greenland

Across the Atlantic

Erik the Red's son, Leif Erikson, was an even greater explorer. Setting out from Greenland, he sailed to what we now call North America. The Vikings called this area Vinland because of all the grapevines that grew there. The Viking homeland in Scandinavia was more than 2,480 miles (4,000 km) away across the Atlantic, making traveling to and from the new land an incredible achievement.

WOW!

To make fire wherever they went, the Vikings collected a type of **fungus** from the bark of trees. They boiled it in urine for a few days, then hammered it into a flammable material, similar to felt. The material was lit using **flint** and steel to create sparks.

Leif Erikson reached North America in around 1000.

TRADE

GENIUS ★ GLOBAL TRADE NETWORK

As the Vikings reached new lands, they came into contact with different peoples and discovered new **natural resources**. It wasn't long before the Vikings realized they could make themselves rich by trading with these countries.

The importance of trade

The **exchange** of goods and ideas became very important in Viking times. Trade helped form relationships with other **cultures** and improved life back home by increasing personal wealth. The Vikings were the leading traders of the time. They traded with cultures in the Middle East as well as with other European **civilizations**.

After the Vikings settled in England, they began issuing coins as the Anglo-Saxons did, although using plain pieces of silver was more common.

(((BRAIN WAVE)))

The Vikings engaged in a type of trade where weighed pieces of silver and gold were used as money. Viking traders had special folding scales to weigh the pieces as accurately as possible.

Trade routes and goods

The Vikings also established trade routes to and from the area that is now Russia, along the Volga River. The goods that the Vikings traded in these areas included timber, wheat, wool, tin, honey, leather, and ivory from walrus tusks. They exchanged these for items such as silver, silk, wine, spices, glass, and pottery.

Trading in slaves

The Vikings were also slave traders, and enslaved people, called thralls, were very valuable. Some enslaved people came from conquered territories in eastern Europe and Britain, but others were Vikings themselves—men and women who had been enslaved as a punishment for committing murder or theft.

A Viking selling an enslaved woman. Traded goods, such as silk and furs, can be seen on the ground.

BATTLE-AXES

The Vikings were a warrior people, and having effective weapons was a matter of life and death. Digging iron from the earth was a complicated process, so only the richest Vikings could afford a full set of weapons and armor.

Weapon wardrobe

A wealthy Viking might own a sword, a spear, and a bow and arrows, as well as a shield, helmet, and armor called **chain mail**. Most Vikings carried much less weaponry than this, but almost all of them owned an ax. They developed axes into useful and terrifying weapons, and used them in imaginative ways!

On the battlefield

Axes started out as simple tools used for chopping wood, but over the years the Vikings adapted them to become weapons. Axes were made larger and wider so they could do more damage. Some battle-axes had a hook, which was used to catch an enemy by his foot or shield before bringing the blade down on him.

The ax was the most common weapon used by the Vikings in battle.

In late Viking times, a large, two-handed ax was invented. This meant the soldier could not hold a shield at the same time. To protect soldiers, the Vikings invented a new battle **tactic**. The soldiers holding the axes would stay behind a front line of warriors, then rush out to surprise the enemy.

SHIELDS

The circular Viking shield was carefully made to provide excellent protection. It was created especially with the Vikings' methods of attack—and defense—in mind.

GENIUS ★ WELL-PROTECTED WARRIORS

Shield construction

Viking shields were about 24 to 38 inches (60 to 97 cm) wide. They were made of seven or eight thin strips of wood. The shields may have been strengthened with iron bands. Viking shields did not have straps to secure them to the soldier's arm. Instead, there was a hole in the middle where an iron handle was attached. An iron dome covered the hole at the front.

The Vikings often hung their shields over the sides of longships. This kept the shields out of the way but still easily accessible. It also protected the sides of the ships from damage by rocks and waves.

Battle tactics

On the battlefield, Viking warriors would form lines of defense. They would hold up their shields so that they overlapped. This created a strong wall that the enemy found hard to break through. The wood that the shields were made from was thin and flexible, making it less likely to be split by a blow from an enemy weapon.

This modern version of a Viking battle shows soldiers with overlapping shields. Viking shields may have been painted with simple patterns.

19

LAW AND DEMOCRACY

The Vikings developed one of the earliest systems of **democratic** government. They made and enforced laws at outdoor meetings called Things, which comes from the Old Norse word *ping*, meaning assembly.

Things

Things were held across Scandinavia and in many other places where the Vikings settled. At a Thing, local landowning men would debate and vote on laws, settle arguments, and judge crimes. Each community had its own Thing. In many ways, Things operated as many modern governments and courts of law do. The word law itself comes from the Old Norse word *lag*.

TEST OF TIME

In 930 in Iceland, the Vikings established Althing, the world's first **parliament**. For two weeks every summer, men gathered to vote and pass laws. Today, the parliament of Iceland is still known as the Althing.

The early Althing was held outdoors in a place now known as Thingvellir, or "Thing Fields," in Iceland.

Feuds and fines

One of the biggest problems in Viking times was the blood feud. This was when the victim of a crime or their family reacted by attacking the person who had committed the crime. Blood feuds could result in years of violence.

To prevent blood feuds, the Vikings introduced fines as a punishment for crimes such as stealing. The local Thing would decide the proper **compensation** for the victim. The Vikings brought this idea to England and France when they settled there, and it soon spread to other parts of Europe. Fines are still a common form of punishment for minor crimes today.

WOW!

Although Viking women were not allowed to vote at a Thing, they enjoyed more freedom than most women at the time. When the men were off exploring or raiding, women ran the farms. They were allowed to own land and could divorce their husbands.

The Jónsbók is the book of Icelandic law, first written in 1281.

LANGUAGE

Many words in the modern English language can be traced back to the Vikings. Their influence can also be seen in many place names where Vikings settled.

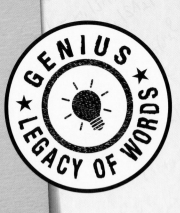

GENIUS ★ LEGACY OF WORDS

Viking words

It is thought that as many as 20 percent of English words come from the Old Norse language. These include many words that begin with "sk," including ski, sky, skin, and skill. Several words that start with the letters "thr" are also of Viking **origin**, such as thrust, thrall, and thrift.

WOW!

Viking and Anglo-Saxon poets used kennings, a word that comes from the Old Norse *kenna*, which means "to know." Kennings describe things as if they were something else. For example, the kennings "whale road" and "bed of fish" both describe the sea.

The Vikings learned words from other languages so that they could communicate with visitors to trading posts, such as the one pictured here.

Place names

As they settled in different areas, the Vikings named their new lands. Many of these places still have the names that show their Viking history. In Normandy, France, the name Normandy comes from the Old Norse words for "land of the northman." In England, places such as Grimsby and Scunthorpe have some of the Old Norse words for "village" or "farm" in their names—*by* and *thorpe*. In Russia, many historians believe the country may have been named after a Viking called Rurik. When he settled in the area, the local people called him *Rus*, which is the **Slavic** word for Viking.

TEST OF TIME

The Vikings named the days of the week after their gods. This influence can be seen in some of the English names.

Sunday: named after Sunni (or Sol), the Norse goddess of the Sun.

Monday: named after Mani, the Norse goddess of the Moon.

Tuesday: named after the Norse god Tyr, who was associated with law and heroism.

Wednesday: named after the chief Norse god Woden, or Odin.

Thursday: named after Thor, the Norse god of thunder, strength, and protection.

Friday: named after Freyja, the Norse goddess of death and love.

Saturday: the Vikings kept the Roman name for this day, named after the Roman god Saturn.

The Norse god Odin was associated with victory, death, and wisdom.

SKIING

Although no one knows for sure when or where people first began to ski, the western tradition of skiing for both enjoyment and transportation has been traced back to early Scandinavian people.

GENIUS ★ IDEAL TRANSPORTATION

Skis helped the Vikings get around more easily in their snowy homeland.

Ancient transportation

Skiing was one of the earliest forms of transportation, and people in Scandinavia have probably skied for around 5,000 years. There are rock carvings in Norway showing people on sleds and wearing skis. However, the Vikings were the first to use modern-style skis and poles.

TEST OF TIME

The word ski comes from the old Norse word *skid*, which means "stick of wood."

24

Skiing gods

The Vikings even worshiped gods who were associated with skiing. For example, Skadi, the goddess of hunting, was often shown skiing with a bow. Ullr, the god of hunting, was usually shown with a bow and skis.

This illustration shows the Norse god Ullr on his skis.

The Reinheimen ski

A 1,300-year-old ski made of birchwood was recently discovered in Reinheimen, Norway. It told experts much more about the Vikings' practice of skiing than they had ever known before. The Reinheimen ski was the first to be found with the **binding** in place. From this, we know that the Vikings made the binding of wicker and leather. We also know roughly how big the Vikings made their skis.

(((BRAIN WAVE)))

Overland travel in Scandinavia was easier in winter than in summer. Then, the Vikings could cross frozen lakes and rivers. Sleds, which experts believe were used to pull **cargo** around in winter, have been found in Viking burial sites.

PERSONAL GROOMING

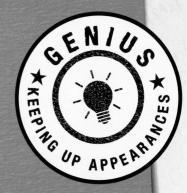

The Vikings have a reputation for being violent, so you wouldn't think they would care much about how they looked. But items found in Viking graves suggest they took personal grooming and hygiene quite seriously.

Many combs found in Viking graves are beautifully decorated, which suggests that they were valued items.

Deer-antler combs

Hair combs have been found in other early cultures, but the Vikings are believed to have been the first to use the type of comb familiar to us today. They were usually made from deer antlers. The Vikings are thought to have worn them on a belt, alongside a sword or knife, and took them when they sailed off on voyages of exploration or raiding.

WOW!

Among the items found in Viking burial sites are tiny spoons thought to be used for scooping wax out of the ears.

Blond is best

The Vikings considered fair hair to be more attractive than dark. To lighten their hair, they washed it in a type of soap made with lye, which acted like bleach. Men also used this special soap on their beards. This treatment may have had the added benefit of getting rid of head lice!

TEST OF TIME

The Vikings wore glasses, making glass lenses out of crushed rock dust. These glasses couldn't have been used to improve eyesight though, so it seems more likely that the Vikings wore them as a fashion statement!

The blacksmith's grave

In 2014, the grave of a Viking **blacksmith** was discovered in Sogndalsdalen, Norway. It contained about 60 different items and revealed a lot about the role and **status** of blacksmiths in Viking society. As well as his weapons and tools, the blacksmith was buried with many personal items. These included a razor, tweezers, scissors for trimming his beard, and a comb made from bone.

Items such as buckles and jewelry found in graves give us a glimpse into the personal habits of the Vikings.

VIKING SAGAS

A saga is a tale that tells of the heroic deeds of Viking families. The Viking sagas cannot be taken as a completely reliable source of information, but they have given us a lot of information about Viking life and culture.

GENIUS ★ LEGENDARY TALES ★

What are the sagas?

The Viking sagas were mostly written in the 1200s and 1300s, but they record events that took place between around 900 and 1000. This was the time when the Vikings were turning away from their **pagan** gods toward **Christianity**.

TEST OF TIME

It has been suggested that the Viking sagas, with their dramatic storylines and larger-than-life characters, are an early form of soap opera!

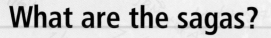

This is a page from the saga called the Flateyjarbok, which includes tales about Icelandic saints and heroes.

28

An epic tale

The Saga of Erik the Red, written sometime before 1265, is mainly about the Vikings' discovery of North America. It describes how Erik was banished from Iceland, then tells how his son Leif Erikson discovered Vinland. Despite its title, the main characters are Thorfinn Karlsefni and his wife Gudrid, who carried on Leif's exploration.

One family's story

Egil's Saga, written around 1240, is a history of Egil Skallagrimsson, who was a farmer and a poet. The saga begins with Egil's grandfather, Ulf, and describes how he and his two sons left Norway for Iceland. The rest of the saga spans 150 years, telling the family's story down to Egil's own children.

WOW!

Most sources that were written during the Viking era describe the Vikings as cruel and bloodthirsty raiders. That's probably because they were written by the victims of Viking raids. The Icelandic sagas present a different side to the Vikings, giving us a more balanced view.

This is a sculpture of Bardur Snaefellsas in Iceland. Bardur, half human and half giant, is the hero of a Viking saga.

GLOSSARY

adapt To change to suit new conditions or surroundings

Anglo-Saxons Early invaders and settlers of England who came from Germany, Denmark, and the Netherlands

archaeological Describes the study of ancient cultures by examining sites and artifacts

binding The part of a ski attached to the flat base that covers the foot

blacksmith Someone who makes objects from iron or steel

capsized When a boat turns over upside down in the water

cargo Goods carried by a ship or vehicle

chain mail Armor made from small metal rings linked together

Christianity A religion based on the teachings of Jesus Christ

civilization The stage of a human society, such as its culture and way of life

colonize To settle in and take political control of another country

compass A device that points north and is used for navigation

compensation Money or goods awarded to someone to pay them back for a loss or injury

confined Forced to stay in a particular place

culture The beliefs and customs of a group of people

democratic Describes a system of government in which people vote and have a say in how things are run

exchange To trade one currency for another

flexible Able to bend or move without breaking

flint A hard type of rock that can be chipped and shaped into sharp objects

fungus A living thing that lives in or on plants, animals, or decaying substances

hull The main part of a ship, including the sides, bottom, and deck

influence To have an effect on something

invention The creation of a new process or device

legacy Something handed down from the past

magnetic Describes something that can pull pieces of metal toward itself

mast A tall upright post on a boat that the sail is attached to

mineral Natural substances that make up rocks, sand, and soil

natural resources Materials or substances from nature that can be used to earn money

navigational Describes something used to provide the correct directions on a journey

Old Norse language A North Germanic language spoken by the Vikings, from about the 800s to the 1200s

origin The point or place where something begins

pagan Describes a religion in which people worship many gods

parliament A group of elected politicians who make laws and represent citizens

pirate A person who attacks and robs ships at sea

raiding To make surprise attacks on people

rivet A metal bolt or pin used for holding wood or metal together

Slavic An eastern European group of people who speak the same language

status A person's level of importance in a society

tactic The planning and organizing of soldiers in war

technology Machinery and equipment developed from the use of scientific knowledge

woven Fabric created by threads crossed together

TIMELINE

700s	Vikings begin to leave their homeland, Scandinavia, and sail along the coasts of Europe
850	Vikings are settling in England
886	King Alfred makes a deal with the Vikings that they can live in an area of England that becomes known as the Danelaw
930	Vikings establish Althing in Iceland
1000	Leif Erikson reaches North America
1066	The Norman invasion of England ends the Viking Age
1200s	The Viking sagas begin to be written

INDEX

Alfred, King of Wessex 5, 31
Althing, the 20
Anglo-Saxons 5, 14, 22, 31

battle-axes 16–17
blood feuds 21

combs 26, 27
compasses 10–11, 12

Danelaw 5, 31

enslaved people 15
Erik the Red 13, 29
Erikson, Leif 13, 29
exploration 8, 9, 10, 12–13, 26

fines 21
fire 13

gods 23, 25, 28
Greenland 13

helmets 4, 16

Iceland 12, 13, 20, 21, 28, 29

kennings 22

language 4, 20, 22–23, 24
laws 20–21
longships 6–7, 8, 9, 12, 18

Oseberg ship 9

raids 5, 8, 9, 31

sagas 28–29
Scandinavia 4, 8, 9, 11, 13, 20, 21, 24, 25
shields 16, 17, 18–19
skiing 24–25
spectacles 27
Svavarsson, Gardar 12

Things 20, 21
trade 5, 9, 10, 14–15, 22

Vinland 13

weapons 16, 17

LEARNING MORE

Websites

www.natgeokids.com/au/discover/history/general-history/10-facts-about-the-vikings/

www.dkfindout.com/us/history/vikings/

www.ducksters.com/history/middle_ages_vikings.php

Books

Higgins, Nadia. *Everything Vikings*. National Geographic Children's Books, 2015.

Raum, Elizabeth. *What Did the Vikings Do For Me?* Heinemann, 2010.

Richardson, Hazel. *Life of the Ancient Vikings*. Crabtree Publishing Company, 2005.